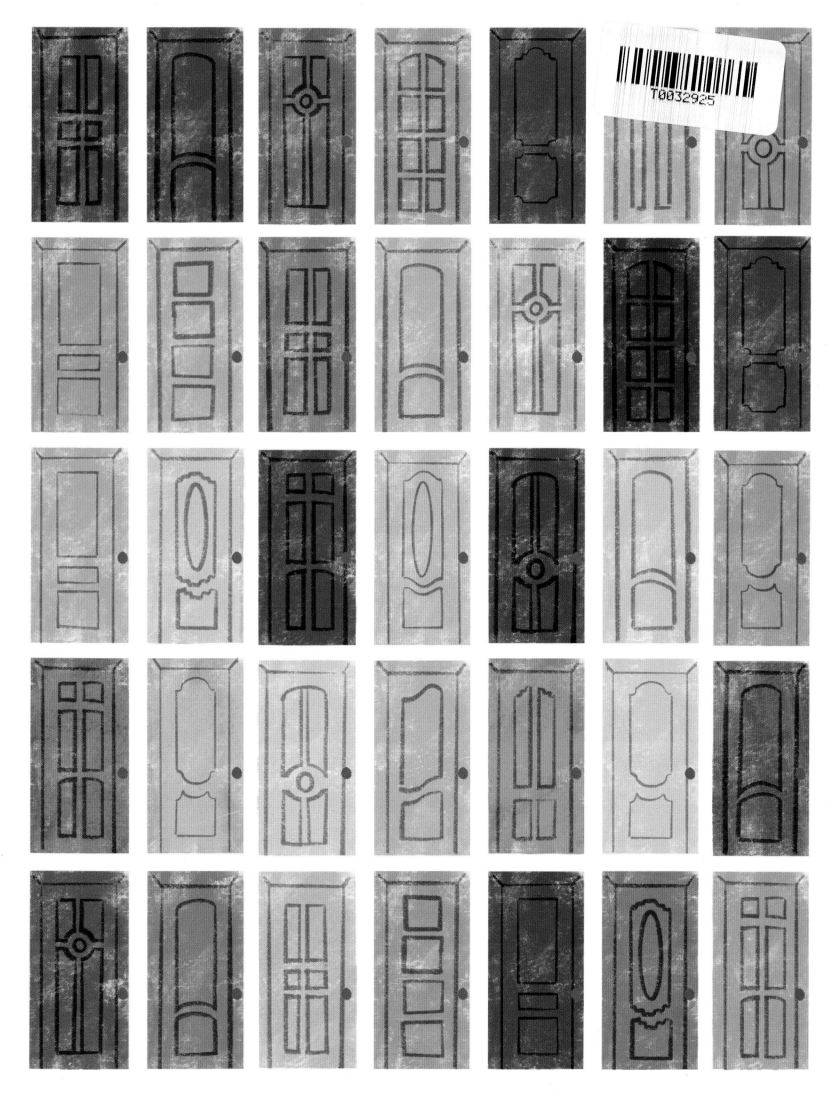

To my dear one, for changing the world just by being yourself. And to N, K, J, and all the tireless trans-rights advocates, for making the world better for everyone. —M.P.

For the kids who see themselves in this book. So glad you are you. —M.M.G.

Text copyright © 2023 by Meeg Pincus
Jacket art and interior illustrations copyright © 2023 by Meridth McKean Gimbel
"A Note from Sarah McBride" copyright © 2023 by Sarah McBride

All rights reserved. Published in the United States by Crown Books for Young Readers, an imprint of Random House Children's Books, a division of Penguin Random House LLC, New York.

Crown and the colophon are registered trademarks of Penguin Random House LLC.

Visit us on the Web! rhcbooks.com

Educators and librarians, for a variety of teaching tools, visit us at RHTeachersLibrarians.com

Library of Congress Cataloging-in-Publication Data
Names: Pincus, Meeg, author. | Gimbel, Meridth McKean, illustrator.
Title: Door by door: how Sarah McBride became America's first openly transgender senator / Meeg Pincus; illustrated by Meridth McKean Gimbel.
Other titles: How Sarah McBride became America's first openly transgender senator
Description: First edition. | New York: Crown Books for Young Readers, an imprint of Random House Children's Books, a division of Penguin Random House LLC, [2023] | Includes bibliographical references. | Audience: Ages 4–7 | Audience: Grades K–1 | Summary: "A picture book biography of Delaware State Senator Sarah McBride"—Provided by publisher.
Identifiers: LCCN 2021027914 (print) | LCCN 2021027915 (ebook) | ISBN 978-0-593-48465-4 (hardcover) | ISBN 978-0-593-48466-1 (library binding) | ISBN 978-0-593-48467-8 (ebook)
Subjects: LCSH: McBride, Sarah—Juvenile literature. | Delaware. General Assembly. Senate—Biography—Juvenile literature. | Transgender legislators—Delaware—Biography—Juvenile literature. | Legislators—Delaware—Biography—Juvenile literature.
Classification: LCC F170.4.M33 P56 2023 (print) | LCC F170.4.M33 (ebook) | DDC 328.73/092 [B]—dc23/eng/20220310

The text of this book is set in 16-point Fairfield LT Std.
The illustrations were created using pencil, watercolor, and Procreate.
Book design by Elizabeth Tardiff

MANUFACTURED IN CHINA
10 9 8 7 6 5 4 3 2 1
First Edition

She didn't understand why her body didn't match her brain and heart.

She didn't understand yet that she was transgender.

All she knew was that imagining telling anyone she was a girl felt like tiptoeing toward a door with angry monsters behind it—and she was too scared to open it.

So, she made a choice. She'd just leave that door closed and be the
boy everyone thought she was.

At least she could try to change the world, if not herself.

DOOR BY DOOR

How Sarah McBride Became America's
First Openly Transgender Senator

by
Meeg Pincus

illustrated by
Meridth McKean Gimbel

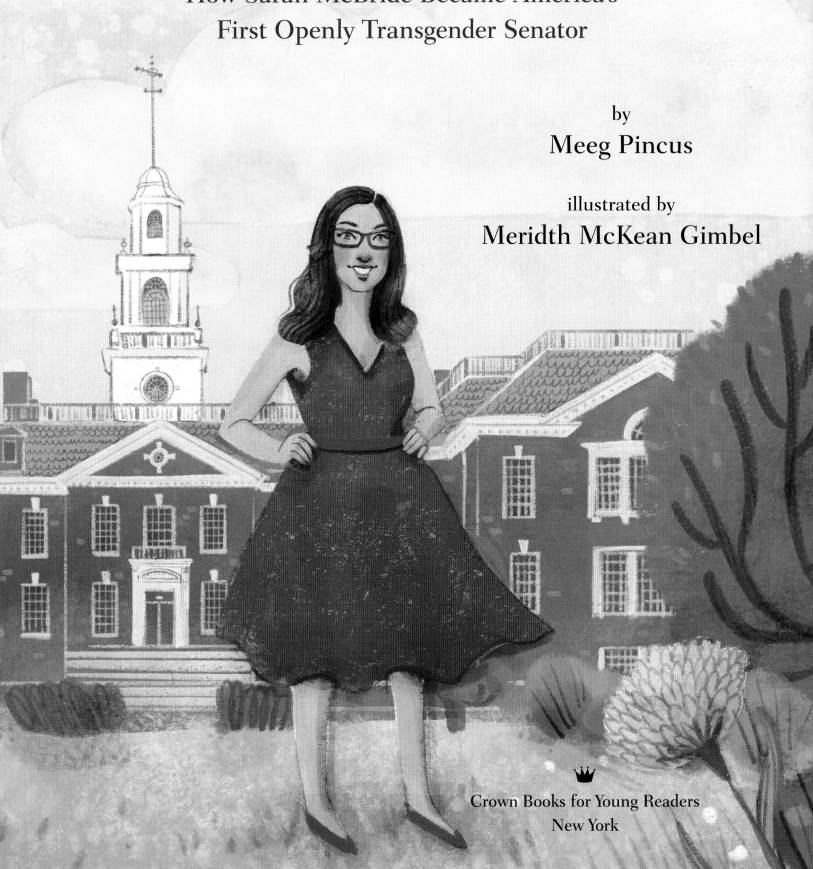

Crown Books for Young Readers
New York

From the time she was a tot, Sarah McBride knew two things
as sure as the trees lining her Delaware street.

One: She knew she wanted to change the world.

Two: She knew who she was inside.

These two truths would shape Sarah's life.

When she first learned about U.S. presidents and all they could do to help people, Sarah felt fireworks in her heart.

Every weekend, she built models of the White House with her blocks.

Every night, she read books about presidents—like Lincoln, FDR, and Kennedy, who used politics and government to take steps toward a more safe, healthy, and equal America.

Sarah knew: *That* was how she'd change the world.

At the same time, Sarah knew who she was inside: a girl.

Problem was, because of the body she was born in, everyone saw and treated her as a boy.

When her teacher separated the class by gender, Sarah pined to line up with the girls.

When playing dress-up with the two sisters across the street, she longed to live in their Cinderella gown.

When she went to bed each night, her belly ached with a feeling like homesickness.
She cried and prayed to wake up as herself.

Worry taunted Sarah: *How could she live both of her truths?*

Everyone loved her as the boy with the sparkling smile, "the little president" in his suit and tie. They might not love her if she wasn't *him*.

Everyone, even her own mom, laughed at TV characters who didn't follow gender rules.

The last thing Sarah wanted was to be a joke— or to be rejected by her family.

One day at her neighborhood pizza parlor, she met her political role model, Delaware's senior U.S. senator.

Her heart felt those fireworks again when he signed a page from his planner to her:

Remember me when you are president!

For Christmas, Sarah asked for a podium to practice
political speeches.

She memorized the inspiring words of a young senator
at a national convention:

We can make sure that every child in America
has a decent shot at life, and that the doors of
opportunity remain open to all!

Sarah knew: That was just what *she* wanted to do.
And politics was her path.

As a teenager, she visited voters, made phone calls, and gave speeches for a candidate for Delaware's governor.

Sarah believed in his vision of helping more people get jobs and education. And he won!

As a college student in Washington, D.C., Sarah became a candidate herself. Running for student body president, she knocked on every dorm room door—thousands of them! She shared her ideas for creating a safer, more welcoming campus for all kinds of students. And she won!

Sarah was living her truth, trying to change the world.

However, her other truth wasn't going away.

Each day of her presidency, Sarah worked hard . . . as the young man everyone saw her as.

But each night, to be able to sleep at all, she had to imagine her entire day again . . . as the young woman she really was.

The homesick feeling had only grown inside her, like a big, dark cloud swallowing the sun.

She was doing the work that she'd dreamed of as a child. But still she cried and prayed to wake up as herself.

Now that she was older, though, Sarah had also learned to do her own research—and had found that she wasn't alone.

She discovered that transgender, or trans, people like her have existed throughout time and cultures.

She saw modern-day trans people of all ages coming out—choosing to live openly as their true gender.

Every hour of every day, she ached to join those brave souls.

The thought made her stomach somersault with fear.

But Sarah knew: That black cloud inside her was ready to burst.

She couldn't live as anyone but her true self any longer.

It was time.

First, she told the most
important people: her closest
friends and family.

It wasn't easy, but, thankfully, they stood by her.

Then, on the last day of her presidency, she prepared to tell the world.
She typed her truth in an online post:

I am transgender. I am a woman. I am Sarah.

She knew: This would determine her future.
With a deep, shaky breath, she clicked "send."

Messages of support poured in to a shocked Sarah.

The university celebrated like it was her birthday (which it kind of was).

Newspapers covered the story—a college campus opening doors for trans people.

Sarah still had a path in politics. She still had family and friends.

And she was, finally, herself.

The sunshine broke through the clouds as she walked into her new life.

As a child, Sarah had built models of the White House.

Years later, she became the first openly transgender person to work there.

As a teen, Sarah had memorized a young senator's political convention speech.

Years later, she became the first openly trans speaker at that same convention.

And that former senator—who'd become President Barack Obama—cheered her on.

In 2020, Sarah knocked on Delaware doors once again, running for state senator. She told residents her ideas to make her home state more safe, healthy, and equal for all. And she won!

Trans kids across the country celebrated their role model's groundbreaking victory.

Sarah's own childhood role model won his election that year, too.

As the U.S. president-elect, Joe Biden mentioned transgender

Americans in his acceptance speech—another first.

Ask Sarah today, and she'll tell you, as sure as
the trees lining her Delaware street:
The two things she knew from the start were true.
But her fear that she couldn't have both was not.

She is Senator Sarah McBride—the woman with the sparkling
smile—opening the doors of opportunity for all . . . and changing the
world in the process.

A NOTE FROM SARAH McBRIDE

Everyone has a story. Each one is filled with setbacks, challenges, hopes, and happiness. All of those stories—what they share and how they are different—make our world interesting and beautiful. And even though each of our stories is different, every story is important because it is someone's. This is my story.

Some of you may be reading this and learning about trans people for the first time. Some of you may have family who are transgender. Some of you may be transgender. No matter who you are, no one is ever too young to learn to be kind, to see the beautiful differences in our world, or to know that you can be yourself and dream big dreams all at the same time.

When I was younger, all I wanted was for my parents to be proud of me, for my friends to be my friends, to do what I love, and to be myself. I was scared it was impossible, and I was worried that what made me different would keep me from doing all the things that bring me joy.

But as I grew up, I saw that the best me was a real me. I learned that if I showed kindness to others, others would be kind to me. I realized that hard times can make us stronger. And I came to believe even more that our differences are our superpowers.

Now, as a grown-up, I'm able to do all that I dreamed of—and I'm able to do it as my authentic self. Today, I know that nothing is impossible. We can be ourselves and reach our dreams.

To anyone reading this book, whether you are transgender or not, know that your story matters. Your voice matters. Your hopes and dreams matter. You matter.

I'm so happy to welcome you on *my* journey with me. I can't wait to see all you do on *your* journey.

Keep dreaming.

SARAH McBRIDE TODAY

In 2020, Sarah McBride became America's first openly transgender state senator, and one of the youngest senators ever to serve in Delaware. Before that, she worked for several years as the national press secretary of the Human Rights Campaign, the country's largest LGBTQ+ civil rights organization, and interned at the White House. Since she came out as trans on her last day as American University's student body president in 2012, Sarah has been living her dream: being fully herself and changing the world through politics and government. But this doesn't mean her life is always easy. She still faces discrimination, from people and laws, like all trans people today. She also lost her beloved husband, trans health care advocate Andrew Cray, to cancer at the young age of twenty-eight. Still, Sarah keeps smiling her well-known smile and doesn't give up. As a state senator, she continues Andy's work fighting for trans people's access to quality health care, and she's passionate about health care for all. She also works hard to make laws protecting equal access to jobs, education, safety, and a clean environment.

AUTHOR'S NOTE

Besides the fact that she's a truly inspiring leader and role model, there are two main reasons I'm passionate about sharing Sarah McBride's story with young readers:

First, because Sarah changed *my* life by sharing her story.

Reading about Sarah in our college alumni magazine in 2012 broke open something in my heart. I was so moved by, and proud of, the campus embracing her. I also realized that, as a cis woman, even though I'd studied gender in graduate school and was working for gay rights, I really didn't know about trans experiences. So I began reading all the life stories I could find by trans authors. I saw common feelings within different lives, and a long history of our culture erasing and harming trans people.

Then a dear loved one tearfully expressed to me feelings about their gender, just like those of the trans authors I'd read. And thanks to those brave stories, starting with Sarah's, I knew what to do: embrace my loved one unconditionally, offer resources, and follow their lead. Since then, I've had the honor of walking alongside my trans loved one on their journey, working with amazing doctors and activists, and becoming an ever-learning advocate in a dedicated, passionate group within the LGBTQ+ community—fighting for trans lives.

Second, because I believe in the power of diverse books for children.

Dr. Rudine Sims Bishop said it best when she wrote that diverse children's books offer mirrors, windows, and sliding glass doors. Kids need to see themselves in books (mirrors), to see others who are different from them (windows), and to imagine walking into the world of someone else (sliding glass doors). According to Dr. Sims Bishop, "Literature transforms human experience and reflects it back to us, and in that reflection, we can see our own lives and experiences as part of the larger human condition."

When we hear someone's story, feel their heart—in life or through a book—it becomes hard to fear or dehumanize them. And we mustn't fear each other. We mustn't fear books. It nourishes children—and all of us—to read many kinds of people's stories, to see common needs and different struggles. Diverse children's books can open space for learning and healing, for compassion and cooperation. They can make us less afraid, less alone, more connected. They can change, even save, lives.

It's not only an honor to work with Sarah on sharing her story with kids through this book, it's part of everything I hope for our children and our future.

KNOW YOUR STUFF:
HOW TO BE A TRANS ALLY AS A CIS PERSON

If you are cisgender, also called cis (meaning *not* transgender, also called trans), here are a few important ways you can support transgender people and be an ally:

Understand that every trans person is unique. Some trans people may express their gender in more typically masculine or feminine ways with their dress or hairstyle. Others may express their gender in more gender non-conforming ways. Some people may describe themselves as trans and/or by other terms like non-binary, gender-fluid, or agender. It's never appropriate to ask someone, "What are you?" If you want to be respectful, you may offer your own name and pronouns and ask, "What about you?" (This means whether a person uses *he/his, she/her, they/their,* or other pronouns.) Your best bet: just ask people their names, listen, and get to know them.

Respect the privacy of trans folks, as you'd want your own respected. Ask them about their interests, favorite books, or movies. Do *not* ask them personal questions about their private body parts, former name, or how they looked before transitioning. These questions can be hurtful and aren't appropriate. (How awful would it feel if someone you just met asked you about your private body parts or something upsetting from your past?) And it's not anyone's place to talk about whether another person is transgender. In fact, sharing this information about someone who is not openly trans could put them in an unsafe situation and cause them real harm. Honor each person's privacy and personal choice about whether, when, or where to discuss their gender identity.

Learn more about trans people in history. Transgender people have existed everywhere throughout time, from ancient cultures to today. But they have mostly been hidden in the United States until recently. There are many notable trans people, past and present, you can learn more about—such as those pictured in this book (We'wha, Candy Darling, Lou Sullivan, James Miranda Barry, Albert Cashier, Alan L. Hart, Lucy Hicks Anderson, Rachel Levine, Willmer "Little Ax" Broadnax, Christine Jorgensen, Billy Tipton, Elliot Page, Renée Richards, Sylvia Rivera, Marsha P. Johnson, Laverne Cox, and Amao Leota Lu). More children's books are coming out every year that share stories of trans history—ask your librarian, teacher, or parent or guardian to help you find them and read them!

Speak out if you hear people saying misinformed or hurtful things about trans people. It makes a big difference to let other cisgender people know that it's not okay to disrespect transgender people, or anyone. Use your voice and privilege as a cis person to show your support for gender diversity and be an ally to trans folks. You can change the world, too!

KNOW YOUR STUFF: POLITICS AND GOVERNMENT

In her youth, Sarah McBride learned everything she could about government—understanding the power and promise of a working democracy. She has used and built on this knowledge to change laws and help others. To understand how government works, you need to know who's who and what's what. Here are a few terms to start with:

Campaign—an organized effort to reach a goal, such as electing someone to a government office

Congress—the lawmaking body of the United States, made up of the Senate and the House of Representatives

Convention—a large meeting of a political party, where members nominate the party's candidates for president and vice president

Democracy—a government in which power is held by the citizens, who freely elect representatives to serve their interests

Election—the organized process of voting for people to serve in government positions

Governor—the head government official of a state

Legislature—the lawmaking body of a U.S. state; in most states, it includes two chambers: a smaller, "upper" senate and a larger, "lower" house or assembly

Mayor—the head government official of a city or town

Politics—the study and activities of government and lawmaking

President—the head government official of a country

President-elect—a newly elected president (there can also be a mayor-elect, governor-elect, etc.)

Senator—a person elected to a senate, the smaller, "upper" lawmaking body of a state or nation

SELECTED BIBLIOGRAPHY

McBride, Sarah. *Tomorrow Will Be Different: Love, Loss, and the Fight for Trans Equality.* New York: Crown Archetype, 2018.

McBride, Sarah. "The Real Me." *The American University Eagle.* May 1, 2012. theeagleonline.com/article/2012/05/the-real-me. (Revised and reprinted in *Huffington Post,* July 9, 2012: huffpost.com/entry/the-real-me_b_1504207.)

McBride, Sarah. 2016 Democratic National Convention Address. July 28, 2016. youtube.com/watch?v=EA9PeYZ7rrI.

McBride, Sarah. Interview with Jennifer Finney Boylan. Strand Book Store. New York City. March 8, 2018. youtube.com/watch?v=NTXdgPKzF6Q&t=64s.

McBride, Sarah. Interview with Rep. Joe Kennedy. Politics and Prose Bookstore. Washington, D.C. March 20, 2018. politics-prose.com/video/tomorrow-will-be-different-sarah-mcbride.

McBride, Sarah. Interview with Seth Meyers. *Late Night with Seth Meyers.* NBC. April 5, 2018. nbc.com/late-night-with-seth-meyers/video/sarah-mcbride-asked-for-a-podium-for-christmas -when-she-was-a-kid/3696499.

Obama, Barack. 2004 Democratic National Convention Address. July 27, 2004. youtube.com/watch?v=ueMNqdB1QIE.

Sims Bishop, Rudine. "Mirrors, Windows, and Sliding Glass Doors." *Perspectives: Choosing and Using Books for the Classroom.* Vol. 6, no. 3. The Ohio State University. Summer 1990.